this is
still life

The Mineral Point Poetry Series

Tanka & Me — Kaethe Schwehn
My Seaborgium — Alicia Rebecca Myers
Fair Day in an Ancient Town — Greg Allendorf
My Tall Handsome — Emily Corwin
A Wife Is a Hope Chest — Christine Brandel
Black Genealogy — Kiki Petrosino
The Rise of Genderqueer — Wren Hanks
This Is Still Life — Tracy Mishkin
Life on Dodge — Rita Feinstein
Calf Canyon — Sarah McCartt-Jackson

The Mineral Point Poetry Series 8 · Kiki Petrosino, Editor

this is still life

poems

Tracy Mishkin

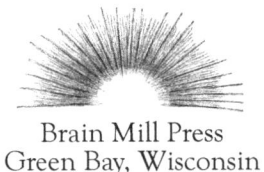

Brain Mill Press
Green Bay, Wisconsin

Some of the poems in this collection have appeared previously in the following publications and are reprinted here with permission:

82 Review: "After Setbacks, We Go Sideways"
Anomaly: "Festival"
Blue River: "End of the World, Part I" (previously titled "A Few Last Words about Us")
Driftwood Press: "The Deadweight Machine"
Great Lakes Review: "What Work Isn't"
Lockjaw: "Stumbling Through" (previously titled "101st Homicide, 2015")
Melted Wing: "Revolution"
Milk Journal: "The Ire Barn"
Off the Coast: "Breed Wisdom"
Panoply: "The Mill Fires Dimmed the Stars" (previously titled "Donora, Pennsylvania")
Raleigh Review: "Making Do"
Slippery Elm: "The Disappeared" (previously titled "Mothers of the Disappeared")
Wabash Watershed: "Vision Problem"

Copyright © 2018 by Tracy Mishkin.
All rights reserved.

Published in the United States by Brain Mill Press.
Print ISBN 978-1-948559-13-3
EPUB ISBN 978-1-948559-16-4
MOBI ISBN 978-1-948559-14-0
PDF ISBN 978-1-948559-15-7

Cover photograph "The Flooded Room (Miniature), 2013" © Yoav Friedlander.
Cover design by Oona Miller.

www.brainmillpress.com

The Mineral Point Poetry Series, number 8.
Published by Brain Mill Press, the Mineral Point Poetry Series is edited by Kiki Petrosino. In odd years, the series invites submissions of poetry chapbooks around a theme. In even years, the editor chooses a full collection.

In Memory of Allen Mishkin

Contents

Foreword by series editor Kiki Petrosino	xi
The Ire Barn	1
When the Corpse Flowers Bloom	2
Vision Problem	3
Malaise	4
Festival	5
America, You Make Me Nervous	6
Burial	7
Flash	8
Fracture	9
What Work Isn't	10
Nostalgia	11
The Deadweight Machine	12
How We Came to Burn Ourselves in Effigy	13
Revolution	14
The Disappeared	15
The Mill Fires Dimmed the Stars	16
Notes from the Goat Rodeo	17
End of the World, Part I	19
This Is Still Life	20
Falling	21
The Art of Distraction	23
Resolution	24
Homecoming	25
Courage	26
After Setbacks, We Go Sideways	27
Making Do	28

Pilgrimage to #StayWoke	29
Breed Wisdom	30
Stumbling Through	31
Author's Acknowledgments	33
About the Author	35

"You turn like a meat wheel full of teeth," Tracy Mishkin's speaker tells a collective "America," and, as readers, we feel the danger made explicit in this vision. Whether the "wheel" symbolizes the grind of our twenty-four-hour news cycle or the seemingly endless circuit of civil unrest around the world, we're caught up, spinning, trying to gain purchase. In *This Is Still Life*, Mishkin has written for America a series of summertime poems, but it's a summer of locusts, of gunshots, and of fires.

The poems in this collection assume a variety of free verse forms, from compact lyrics of a single stanza ("How We Came to Burn Ourselves in Effigy") to tersely sectioned sequences ("Notes from the Goat Rodeo") to richly textured prose poems ("Resolution"). The pieces are bound by Mishkin's inimitable voice, whose laser-like attention to the minutiae of our fallen world creates an immersive reading experience.

In these poems, the burial of a family cat is the last ceremony of civility before everything falls apart ("I laid a sprig of cherry blossoms on top of the box. The first shovelful knocked it aside."). Despair itself, personified as an unwelcome houseguest in the basement ("Resolution"), tries to convince the speaker to give up hope ("[T]here are no more leaves to turn over / No new bottles of wine."). The speaker inhabits, and we inhabit, an exhausted landscape whose former abundance has given way to violence, anxiety, and fatigue.

So where, in the midst of ruin, does a poem find fixity? Through which slender crack of light can language thread its hopeful vine? In *This Is Still Life*, there's still power in human connection, in our capacity for love. Two friends "dash through urban gullies." A married couple prepares dinner, walks the dog, stays woke. Each small sign of community has the potential to lead us out of the dark wood.

"On foot, by bike, we take / this earthen path next to the canal

/ until it forks, up to the road," Mishkin's speaker tells us in a poem about pilgrimage. The terrain we need to traverse to reclaim our moral center requires strenuous effort and firm resolve. "We travel here to be reminded / of our faith," the speaker observes, and we sense that it is the poet's continued faith in humanity that could stop the deadly spinning of this wheel. I hope so.

Read *This Is Still Life* for the astonishing way it braids darkness and light. Read these poems for hope in a broken time. Whatever your reasons, read these poems. And do it now.

Kiki Petrosino
Editor, Mineral Point Poetry Series

The Ire Barn

I don't want to go inside. It smells of dark
and heat and rotting grass. Here a man can
hold the trigger and spill. Smash the gas pedal
and kill. All this red, like a vine tightening
on my neck. Kids strapped in car seats feel
the water already at their knees. Someone
is trying to pray, but the words leak out
like bright arterial blood. A snarling dog bites
the air with the flat crack of breaking glass.
The token embrace that doesn't stop the hate.
I think this place goes on forever. I don't want
to go inside, but I'm already here.

When the Corpse Flowers Bloom

This is the summer our son works his first job,
and we walk with a tiny swagger until we turn
on the radio. This is the semi-automatic summer
of trucks crushing children, of shooting
& moving until we're cornered and the cops
send in a juggernaut to kill us by remote control.

This is the summer we pace the neighborhood,
current events detonating around us. Two people
sleep in a car with a backseat toddler, her fist
crammed in her mouth, as our son did when he lost
sight of us. Two people who might not be sleeping.
The woman's skin a little blue. The man sagging.

This summer we hear yes more than no,
our heads held high until the news breaks
over us like a salty wave. It's the summer of our last
presidential election, of finding out how long
we can hold our breath, how much
is more than we can take.

Summer those pungent corpse flowers bloom,
summer of church-sponsored needle exchanges,
summer that renders quaint the '90s bowl
of free condoms. Summer of undertow.
We swim parallel to shore, as we were taught.

Vision Problem

Retinal floater drifting
like a jellyfish. Doctor says
come back if it's worse.
Come back if you see flashes.
If you wake up blurry, come back.
If you don't see color, come back.

If you only see color.

If it was his fault because
he didn't bring a gun to church. Her fault
whites were outnumbered
at the pool. If he looked like
he had a gun. Played with a toy
gun. Slept in the wrong house.
In the wrong neighborhood. If
six foot four, three hundred pounds.
Mentally ill. Asthma. Accent.
If walking in the street.
On the sidewalk.

If he ran.

Malaise

I used to capsize my canoe for fun,
stop dogs with a word. Now life skates
past me. I push down on one end and the other rises.

In Vegas, I overcame my fear of heights.
Now my luck runs down and out.
I'm a scratch-off blowing through the parking lot.

I used to read the book of bad dreams and shrug.
Now I smell metal when a storm is miles away.

I used to say, "There's always room for you
around my table." Now the neighbors cut
their eyes at me. I say, "People die. Get used to it."

I used to find connectors in a land
of cul-de-sacs. Now nobody rides for free.

I thought that running water changed the world
more than earthquakes.
Grief has made me a dry well.

I was a cornucopia. Inverted,
I'm an empty crow bag.

Festival

Break the fast with figs
and dates at sundown.

Set rows of oil lamps
on the new moon night.

Join a fertility rite
where everyone wears a mask.

~

At our wedding, I circle you seven times.
A plain gold band. Seven blessings.
You are beaming.

Our son calls from college, asks us to sing
the ancient words with him. Before we finish,
he is crying.

America, You Make Me Nervous

You turn like a meat wheel full of teeth.

A third of your people believe
only Christians are truly American.

I have considered jumping
ship.

I try to catch my breath,
but you start up again, America,
pitching bricks from the overpass.

The night will not stop burning.

America, I'm sewing twenties
into my dresses. America,
take a good look at yourself.

My father prays in the forest
where his grandmother was shot.

Burial

The gray cat curled carefully in a shoebox, her flesh hardened by death. The man began two holes, abandoned them filled with spring rainwater. As he dug the third, his foot smashed a pile of dog crap. The box went in the grave. We didn't speak.

The way she followed him around as a kitten, watched him fix the sink. The round red bed she slept in: first atop the dresser, then under the table when she could no longer leap. The drawer of widowed socks, their mates lost under beds.

I laid a sprig of cherry blossoms on top of the box. The first shovelful knocked it aside. More dirt slapped the cat casket. Clods and crumble, a mound rose. He patted my back, wiped his boots. I went inside, vacuumed every trace.

Flash

I used to paint on canvas torn
from the earth. My hands brushes,
flinging color across the room.
Art all night, days running with dogs,
digging inspiration from dumpsters.

But I quit the gutwork, swerved
to gimmick and shine. Polished
where I should have tarnished.
Brandished the brush like a designer purse.

My sheets an angry tangle, I spun around.
The sky ran in the rain. Even as I fell,
the critics said I'd never flown higher.
Rice fired from cannons at the marriage
of hot and new. My heart in shards.

I'm a box of ash. All the passion
hasn't come back. Dandelion fluff
blowing through my hands. Tiny ghosts.

Fracture

Dolled up in camouflage, unremarkable
citizens, we fire only when provoked.

Everything provokes us. Bloody gravel
in the alley. A child's shoe. We aim at strangers
and neighbors until the morgues give up.

The streets grow slick and silent, the leaves
skitter and flinch. We learn to use a knife
to open cans. One day of mourning spills
into another. We leave the flags at half-mast.

What Work Isn't

You're building a machine that turns everything
into a joke. Pallets, clotheslines, odd bits
of hose. Every project half-finished or never quite
begun. How is sodden carpet worth saving?

I yank weeds, snatch black plastic mats, and load
the wheelbarrow again. Sweat spatters my glasses.
When rain comes, I slog on. Junk limps
into the dumpster—bricks and rakes and bones
the dog has long abandoned.

When I ask for help, you say the grass is wet
and you are wearing sandals. Your asthma is acting up.
You fell asleep on the couch. You late
and lazy bastard. I should throw you in that dumpster,
change the locks, and make love to the silence.

Nostalgia

Remember when poems were printed on bath towels? When artists painted landscapes on the cheeks of children in the park? When presidents weren't afraid to cry? Remember the lampposts glowing with invitations to celebrate Diwali? When we opened our homes to travelers? Every department store had hunchback mannequins. There was no getting canned when you gave two weeks' notice, no juggling the work of three—for half the pay you had before. No pirates raiding pension funds. We had bald-faced fun raking old ladies' yards. Pillow shams were real. Every book had a large-print edition. And we recognized ourselves in the illustrations.

The Deadweight Machine

As if a tectonic shift has dumped a mountain
on his chest, my husband slumps in the easy chair.
Five weeks until the homeowners insurance
drops us, stacks of useful junk around the yard.
The deadweight machine measures how you hold up
against tension and compression.

When he begins to snore like Rip Van Winkle,
I imagine an organic grocer's typo has created
a display of orgasmic blueberries. I eat them all
without paying. A man in a green apron restocks
the shelves with tender hands.

Before the war, people weighed beginning again
in a new language against the coming storm.
Every time I think of leaving, he catches a death
rattle in my car, stops the house from flooding,
sweet-talks a raccoon out the kitchen door.

How We Came to Burn Ourselves in Effigy

Each dawn brought new reports
of indifference. We shot ourselves
in the foot, reloaded. When laughter
stopped working, we managed anger
like pain. The escalators sucked us in
by our shirttails and nobody stopped
to help. We slept ten hag-ridden hours
and woke exhausted. White-knuckled coffee
and the wheel. Drove past the broken windows
of the Church of the Resurrection.
The last gay bar. We were ordered to jerk
the baby from her mother's breast.
To send children into the crossfire.
When a man ran from us, we shot him in the back.

Revolution

You are a spinning top, jerking
from one pleasure to the next.

I am a searchlight on a watchtower
longing for the ground.

You want the waves in California
to want you. I am green
as sea glass.

I want to paint naked men.
Please touch me. Please
just leave.

The Disappeared

the sun seeps
under the blindfold

the soldiers hold
fire

Her children are deer
who have taken corn
from a trembling hand,
then flashed across the yard.

bodies thrown from planes
rise

If they returned on a rainy night,
like a comet gone
for centuries, she would ask
no questions.

The Mill Fires Dimmed the Stars

When my father was eleven,
a warm air mass trapped
fluorine and sulfuric acid
in the valley. The town sank
under thick yellow smog.

The fire chief begged oxygen
from nearby towns, steered
by scraping the curb.

The furnaces of the Zinc Works
and the Steel & Wire plant
raged all four days. The owners saw
no reason to shut down.

My father walked on tin can stilts
across his mother's just-washed floor.
Outside, fine grit sifted into his lungs.
Folks in surgical masks passed him
and he waved.

My father was a paper boy in acid rain.

Notes from the Goat Rodeo

I.
with you, it's drought or deluge

the leaves fall one by one
until the plant is only a stem

II.
regarding your suffocating generosity
I repeat
my fish, my decision

III.
valleys are depressions
between bright mountains

I cannot see
the foothills

IV.
crawling through the cave
I scrape my shoulders

as the passageway narrows
my throat closes

V.
ten thousand years before a stalactite crashes down

heavy trash day doesn't come
often enough

VI.
seeking a way out, I hold up
a candle, hoping for a breeze flicker

I remember rain that fell so hard
the world changed

VII.
the things we box up
blow open

tires in shreds
on the highway

VIII.
stop talking
just stop

it's quiet in here
the fish have no eyes

End of the World, Part I

Though the gutters ran with the waters of Prozac, it was not nearly enough. We stayed at jobs we never should have taken. In marriages of stale convenience. We avoided the eyes of friends. Thought we'd gotten used to catcalls, to being ridiculed or ignored. No sleep for weeks made us thick and slow. We couldn't take the stairs. Confused one kind of hunger for another. Forgot how to breathe without a cloud of smoke. Neglected the art that sustained us. Our cars glass caskets, we all drove the same streets.

This Is Still Life

The house has a fresh coat of pain.
Screwdriver and utility knife abandoned
on the bed. Drawers choked
with plastic forks. Receipts, seeds,
and batteries. Needles, carpet tacks,
an open blade. Red string streaming
from cabinets—the battle flag
of a man who throws nothing away.

I should have split when I first saw
his apartment, crammed with power tools
and old TVs. Barely space to sleep.
But we weren't sleeping, we were burning.
Falling. More room in my heart
for crazy than I knew.

My mother knows I'd rather get wet
than wait. She warns me not to fight
to reach the items on the highest shelf.
Lightning isn't fair, she says. Arugula
doesn't make it healthy. When you need
a Phillips, all you find are flatheads.
She calls my house *memento mori*:
orchids, bonsai, sun-bleached boards.

Falling

I.
So much rain had fallen
we had begun to curse the ants
while crushing them.

Emptiness rose like floodwaters.
We were dull leaves plummeting.
We were mold stinking in floorboards.

We tried saying everything
we thought. We voted
as a bloc.

We were icy slices of potato plunging
into the fryer. We should have known
we would explode.

II.
We the people whose jobs float away.
The sun returns. FEMA comes and goes.
The jobs stay gone.

We trade prescription drugs for back-to-school clothes.
It is so easy. And when we get clean—oh, the other
mothers, the voices in our heads.

III.
I let the children down gently
from the bus I drive, then settle in my car
to wait the hours out between the coming
and the going home. Talk radio, speak
to my heart of all that I have lost.

The Art of Distraction

Neither of us cheats. We steal
only time from each other.

We are behind
the chains. We spin free.

You are the pain in the base
of my thumb. I am the ache
in your knees.

We skulk past the household things
stacked in the sink. Glasses lodged
under heavy pans. A spoon
in the disposal.

You sprawl on the couch, the dog's head
on your crotch.

We can't ride together
without arguing. We can
continue like this.

Resolution

In the basement that still scares me, Despair is lying on the pool table, resting his head on the eight ball. I've come down for another bottle of Merlot, carrying the list of my daily failures—lucky me, it's still under a page. Despair speaks a language whose rhythms I recognize and almost understand. His accent glossy and ruthless. I'm wearing the T-shirt that says I Do Not Need Another Cat. More advice I've ignored. Despair is sporting my purple velour shirt from the '70s, but he might as well be head to toe in black. I resolve to temper my boiling heart, learn to count to three, count myself among my allies. But the people I know are moral chameleons, trading so hard in penny emotion that the stars ache in the heavens. I cut the lights, but Despair sees better in the dark than I do. Whispers that there are no more leaves to turn over. No new bottles of wine. I tell myself I'll chew over my words before they ooze from my mouth. Tape my lips to mask the slips. I don't care if it breaks all the rules.

Homecoming

I wish we were making brownies, scraping batter
into the pan, licking the spatula. Baking time
is for sinking into a novel, my thigh touching yours,
the dog's blunt head on my lap.

All this I picture while driving home from ten hours
listening to people's fears and needs, and the wanting
is so strong I can hear the dog sighing, though
when she sighs, it's from happiness.

I tell myself you're making dinner from scraps
of cast-off meals, spinning brussels sprouts into soup.
If so, I'll smell the garlic as I leave the car and greet
the half moon, who's stamped on the night like a smile.

Courage

The massacres continue, only a few
averted. A young father who wakes early
to pray sees someone charging
the mosque shouting, "God is great."
Adel tackles a man wrapped in death.
His widow wakes happy: he is a martyr.
Yet how little of him remains.

~

Despite the blisters in her mouth,
the baby smiles. Her flower headband covers
a red sore. Skin so fragile they call it
butterfly. The layers slide against each other,
swelling, tearing. Lilah wants to sit and crawl.
Her mother changes bandages, bares
bubbled flesh. Imagines her child's knees
rubbing the carpet.

~

I chew bones and heave until empty, dream
of a hand reaching for mine. Hand without
a weapon. Hand that won't hurt.

I'm a nail, yes. But you don't
always have to be a hammer, world.

After Setbacks, We Go Sideways

We dash through urban gullies, thistles swiping our legs. We've lost the stone head. The old man on the three-wheeled bicycle shouts that courage is a broken rake still gathering leaves. The flat sandstone face stood two hundred years. Until graffiti on the covered bridge. Until slurs on the church. We catch our breath, find healing goldfish in the middle of obligation and the clock. Somewhere, the stone head endures. At night, we nestle in a drawer of odd socks, a ray of yes in a world of no.

Making Do

I sprawled on the couch. When you climbed
the stairs at ten, I said I was not tired.
I read until I grew lonely for my pillow.

The hills ran with burning rain, the rubble
of discarded hearts. We were blue marble,
streaked with regret, a banquet of ants at the bone.

You cooked odd meals, walked dogs without a leash.
I worked long hours, watched a man who dragged
his leg struggle over icy sidewalks. Some nights
I didn't even call to say I would be late.

But see, I have restrung the loom, layered
other colors with the beige of this life.
Now texture, depth. Shadows that curl like lace.
In January the sun comes closest to the earth.

Pilgrimage To #StayWoke

On foot, by bike, we take
this earthen path next to the canal
until it forks, up to the road
and down to the water, where
the bridge blocks the sun,
a quiet place where we can best
remember how to feed hope.
Yes, it's graffiti on a bridge, but
the cleaning crew will nod
and leave it up, knowing
we travel here to be reminded
of our faith.

Breed Wisdom

The pit bull knows how strong she is.
Not bothered by a bit of rot, she lips
apple from my hand, dirt on her chin
from nibbling grass. She knows when
to chomp, to nip—and how to close
her jaws gently when the ball shifts
and my fingers slip into her mouth.
Her tongue is generous. She knows
the song of anticipation, the smell
of woodsmoke on a cold spring day.
She nudges me from obsession,
nose on my wrist. She knows stillness
and the time for speech.

Stumbling Through

After the yellow tape and the dark blood,
after the wallet with our family photos
is released, after three days of paid bereavement
pass and the jar goes round at work
for casket funds, after I dream of identifying
the body, after the cops come back
to question us again, after praise for the Lord
and the embalmer's skill, after whispers of revenge
and *today we do not mourn*, then the first breath
without a sob.

Author's Acknowledgments

This chapbook began as my MFA thesis at Butler University, which I completed in 2017 under the capable direction of Alessandra Lynch and David Shumate. I'm grateful to them and to my classmates, especially Mark Lilley and Hannah Sullivan Brown, and to the members of my writing group, InterUrban. Amelia Martens provided excellent feedback in her manuscript consultation.

My gratitude goes to Kiki Petrosino and Brain Mill Press for publishing this chapbook, in which I have tried to share different voices of our times and the importance of listening to them. You are "a ray of yes in a world of no." So we all must be.

About the Author

Tracy Mishkin is a call center veteran with a PhD and a graduate of the MFA program in creative writing at Butler University. She is the author of two previous chapbooks, *I Almost Didn't Make It to McDonald's* (Finishing Line Press, 2014) and *The Night I Quit Flossing* (Five Oaks Press, 2016). She has been nominated twice for a Pushcart—both times by Parody—and published in *Raleigh Review* and *Rat's Ass Review*.

www.ingramcontent.com/pod-product-compliance
Lightning Source LLC
Chambersburg PA
CBHW041314110526
44591CB00022B/2913